SAMYE

IN MEMORIAM

Pema Drimed
Pema Wangyal of Dolpo
and
Venerable Lobpon Pema Gyelsten

SAMYE

A PILGRIMAGE TO THE BIRTHPLACE
OF TIBETAN BUDDHISM

MIKEL DUNHAM

FOREWORD BY HIS HOLINESS THE DALAI LAMA

JODERE
GROUP

CIP data available from the Library of Congress

ISBN 1-58872-083-7
07 06 05 04   4 3 2 1
First printing, March 2004

Editorial supervision by C H A D   E D W A R D S

Art direction by C H A R L E S   M C S T R A V I C K

Book design by J E N N   R A M S E Y

J O D E R E   G R O U P ,   I N C .
P.O. Box 910147
San Diego, CA 92191-0147
800.569.1002
www.jodere.com

A   H E A R T F E L T   T H A N K S   T O :

Gudu Lungstub and Goser and LO—three times thank you. Bonnie Solow, superlative friend, agent with the magic wand; Debbie Luican, mellow conjurer of books; Sindu Muchu, Beth, Sandra, David, Ron, Matt and Tina Miller, Laura, Kim, Jyamyang, Roger E. McCarthy, Jampa, Romanos, Chris Byrne, Jessica Samples, Chad Edwards, and Charles McStravick—all, in their own way, leavened the mix or smoothed the way.

Finally, to my wife, Margaret, and to our sons, Adrian and Zachary, my love and gratitude for everything you bring to this life.

CONTENTS

THE DALAI LAMA

FOREWORD

Samye holds an immensely important place in Tibetan hearts and minds, because, when it was founded by Padmasambhava and Santaraksita from India in the year 770, it was the first Buddhist monastery in Tibet. Buddhism had already begun to spread in the Land of Snow, but during Padmasambhava's stay it became firmly established. At this time the translation of Buddhist literature from Sanskrit into Tibetan began, and a section of the monastery was given over to its pursuit. With the ordination of the first seven Tibetan monks at Samye, the monastic tradition so important to the flourishing of the practice and teachings of Buddhism began there too. Thus, we consider Samye the place where the establishment of Buddhism in Tibet took firm root.

In addition to representing the origin of a considerable legacy, even the buildings themselves are significant. On the one hand they are said to have been modelled on the plan of the great Odantapuri temple in India, on the other, being constructed in the form of a three-dimensional mandala, they represent the universe as it is described in Buddhist cosmology. Over the course of time they came to house marvellous collections of scriptures, paintings, statues and other religious images. When I was still in Tibet, I dearly wanted to visit Samye and see these wonders with my own eyes, but the opportunity never presented itself. The closest I came was when I crossed the Tsangpo (Brahmaputra) river nearby in a yak skin coracle during my escape in 1959. Sadly we were then in too much of a hurry to stop and pay our respects.

After that, with the Chinese occupation of Tibet and the ensuing Cultural Revolution, Samye suffered substantial harm. The buildings were devastated, religious images were defaced, smashed or removed and great numbers of irreplaceable books were destroyed. The resident monks were expelled and their places were taken by cattle. Subsequently, enthusiastic renovation has taken place and Samye has been restored to something of its former splendour.

Today, it is once more the focus of pilgrimage as people come from all over Tibet and abroad to pay tribute to the long tradition of teaching, practice and realisation that Samye continues to represent. I welcome this book of photographs that seeks to convey the impression that Samye makes on pilgrims as they approach and make their way round the monastery. For those of us who are unable to go there ourselves, this is a valuable and moving substitute.

March 27, 2003

PART I

BUILDING THE INCONCEIVABLE

King Trhisong Detsen.

BON: THE PRE-BUDDHIST RELIGION OF TIBET

TIBET'S RUGGED TERRAIN profoundly informed Bon, the ancient religion of Tibet. The Bonpos, Tibet's native inhabitants, played host to the highest mountains in the world. Death-defying gorges, vast expanses of isolation at 14,000 feet or more, temperature swings that could soar or plummet 80 degrees within a single day, gale-force winds, mountain passes prohibited by snow, scant rainfall coupled with the briefest of agricultural growing seasons—all of these climatic and topographic hardships influenced the Bonpos' outlook on the realm of the gods. The resultant religion was animistic and shamanistic: The sun, moon, mountains, lakes, rivers, planets, and comets were deified; trees were mystical power sources; wild beasts could be personal emissaries of gods or goddesses; and the Bonpos regarded waterfalls and singular rock formations as anthropomorphic and therefore worthy of reverence.

It was a heavily populated pantheon, largely hostile to the human race. Benevolent gods did exist but there was a predominance of evil deities engaged in an internecine struggle for power. Humans, of whom the gods were jealous, were caught up in the maelstrom. Appeasing vindictive gods was the primary way in which to avoid pestilence, infertility, famine, and madness. Exorcism, the constructions of "spirit traps," divination, the preparations of poisons, sorcery, ophiolatry, cannibalism, and human sacrifice were among the conciliatory rites lavished on the stronghold of the demon world—a world of fire and terrifying monsters.

To outsiders, Tibetans resembled their gods in so much as they were a feared warrior race—both brutal and unpredictable. *King Gesar,* Tibet's epic folk tale, which dates back well before the introduction of Buddhism, documents a Tibet that "was not just barbarous, but savage in the extreme. There is continual talk of eyes being torn out, of blood being drunk from skulls, of tortured enemies, of trophies consisting of parts of the human anatomy offered to victorious kings."[1]

Like King Gesar, Tibetan monarchs were generals. When they triumphed on the battlefield, it was because the Bonpo gods were with them. But it went further than that: Tibetan kings were gods. The first monarch had descended from heaven by a rope; all of his descendants were worshipped both during their lifetimes and after their deaths. A cult developed not unlike the Egyptian worship of dead pharaohs. "The body of the dead king was first anointed with gold dust and then placed in the center of nine enclosures. A golden image of the king was seated upon a throne, which was surrounded by silver, gold, turquoise, and other treasures. An elaborate ritual guided the spirit of the dead king safely to the other world and provided for his needs along the way."[2] The cemetery of the kings, located in the Yarlung Valley, was sacred ground and the tombs of the kings were "guarded by special ministers of the interior. These guards were assigned to the tomb for the rest of their lives and were not permitted to interact in any way with other people . . . the tombs became important retreat centers and were symbolically connected with the passing of royal power to the next generation."[3]

As will be seen, this unbroken lineage of god-kings, supported by a Bonpo ministry, would create a major obstacle for the establishment of Buddhism.

The initial appearance of Buddhism probably transpired during the reign of King Lha Thothori Nyentsen.[4] Late in his reign, two Indian panditas, intent on promulgating Buddhism, crossed the Himalaya and presented the Bonpo ruler with a book of Buddhist scripture. The Indians' mission was a failure. They "found that the king could neither read, nor understand the meaning. So the scholar and translator returned [to their homeland]".[5] Nevertheless, the illiterate god-king regarded the gift as an auspicious blessing and named the mysterious book *The Awesome Secret.* "Not wanting his ministers to know that the book had come from India, the king told them it had descended from the sky and that he had been shown in a dream that" eventually, a Tibetan

The wrath of Bonpa deities.

king would reign who could read Sanskrit and reveal the secret.[6]

Centuries passed.

Militarily, it was a triumphant time for Tibet. By the seventh century A.D., a succession of powerful warrior-god-kings had transformed the tribal realm into one of Asia's major armed forces. Borders reached China in the east, Kokonor in the north and Magadha, India in the south. But the Bonpo nation was illiterate and ill prepared to be regarded in the same league of sophistication as its Buddhist neighbors. The monastic universities in India, the Chinese patronage of *Chan* (later known as "Zen" in Japan), the spread of Buddha's doctrine along the Silk Road—all signaled the apogee of Buddhist thought and culture in the East so that, when Tibet burst onto the international scene, it found itself to be "an island in the midst of a Buddhist sea."[7]

The situation changed with the arrival of King Songtsen Gampo (circa 618–49 A.D.), one of the great rulers of ancient Tibet. He was only 13 when he assumed the throne. Still, he proved to be an irrepressible leader. His success as a general was matched by his thirst for knowledge and organizational skills. He centralized his government and transferred the capital from Yarlung to Lhasa. His marriages to Nepalese and Chinese princesses—both ardent Buddhists—had a profound impact on Tibetan history. The queens brought Buddhist statuaries from their respective countries that are revered above all images in Tibet to this day. They also imported Buddhist scriptures and introduced "the first rudiments of Buddhist worship"[8] to the king, just enough to whet his appetite and leave him yearning for more, which, in turn, instigated his mandate that a written language be created for the Tibetan people.

King Songtsen Gampo assembled a delegation and sent them to India to study grammar and writing with the ultimate goal of formulating a national alphabet. The result was "an ingenious and elegant lexicon that was elaborated on the model of Brahmi and Gupta script and not too far removed from the Sanskrit used in Indian classic texts."[9] The king then commissioned a translation program led by an international Buddhist team who collaborated with Tibetan translators. Eight treatises on Tibetan grammar were written.[10] The king himself translated the *Awesome Secret* into Tibetan, thereby fulfilling a prophecy by his ancestor, King Lha Thothori Nyentsen, that the unintelligible Indian book would one day be revealed—an act held in such high esteem that in the twentieth century, Tibetan currency notes were dated in so many years from its arrival.[11]

With a written language available, the sciences of astronomy and medicine began to flourish. Cultural influences poured in from all directions. The study of Indian and Chinese painting styles was introduced. Art and architecture bloomed. The king constructed temples, including the Jokhang, the central cathedral of Lhasa, to house his wives' Buddhist statuary and other holy artifacts.

The king also drafted the first code of law and moral conduct, as well as the first histories of Tibet. Finally, he established an institution described as "the twin system of temporal and spiritual authority" with the monarch himself embodying this authority—a system followed all the way up to the present Dalai Lama.

Still, the degree to which Buddhism took root was negligible. In spite of the king's concerted efforts, the Bonpo aristocracy resolutely balked at conversion. Sanctioning translations from India was one thing, getting rid of their Bonpo gods was quite another. The shamans fought Buddhist influence, particularly in matters of liturgical practices. And perhaps most significantly, King Songtsen Gampo failed to create a monastic system in which schools could support mass conversion. Buddhism remained a private club within the king's immediate household.

Several generations of warrior-kings transpired. Tibetan borders continued to expand. The Bonpo status quo remained unchanged.

Architecture blooms: King Songtsen Gampo orders the construction of the Jokhang in Lhasa.

TRHISONG DETSEN, THE GREAT BUDDHIST KING

THEN CAME THE REIGN OF KING TRHISONG DETSEN (circa 755–797 A.D.). He was Tibet's greatest general and political tactician. His brilliant incursions into foreign territories absorbed most of Central Asia. From Afghanistan, northern Pakistan, Nepal, and India to the Chinese provinces of Sichuan and Gansu, King Trhisong Detsen's colonization was invincible. (For a brief period in 763 A.D., his troops even occupied the Chinese capital at that time—present day Xian). In every sense of the word, this king was an emperor.[12]

He was also a Buddhist, which created, on the home front, a far more challenging battlefield.

Prior to his assumption, a law had been enacted prohibiting the practice of anything other than Bon. The power elite actively persecuted Buddhist transgressors.[13] To make matters more difficult, King Trhisong Detsen assumed the throne as a teenager—no small challenge for a boy who wished to wrench away the reins of religious power. In an effort to gain better understanding of the political intrigue and religious tug-of-war within his inherited government, he familiarized himself with the minutia of the Bonpo tradition. He also pored over the biographies of his father and grandfather[14] and diagnosed the generational patterns of resistance within the ruling class.

Shantarakshita, the great Indian scholar brought to Tibet by King Trhisong Detsen.

Here was the problem: As a god-king, the security of his sacred status hinged on the Bonpos' *belief* in him. How could he eliminate Bon without renouncing the support system for his divine attributes, the very key to his kingly unassailability?

Continually expanding the Tibetan borders must have helped his political positioning but, in a religious struggle, sheer belligerence would not be the answer. A religious battle would require: 1) secret conscription of the few Buddhist sympathizers already within the aristocracy, and 2) the exploitation of Bon mysticism.

Trhisong Detsen's first strike was to take the Bonpos' worshiping of dead kings, amplify it, and then use it against them: "There were two junior ministers who were willing to help the king . . . . They approached various sympathetic ministers, apprising them of their intention . . . . Then they bribed an oracle to predict a great famine and epidemic for the country and a short life for the king unless two loyal subjects submitted to self-imposed exile to the royal cemetery as a sacrifice for the welfare of the king and the country."[15]

In front of the assembled ministry, these two junior ministers volunteered themselves for the sacrifice. The two senior ministers—the most conservative of the Bonpo ruling class—"seeing that this could result in loss of face for them, voiced a protest and insisted that not only were they the senior ministers, but they were of greater loyalty than anyone else; therefore, they should be given the honor of going into exile. The assembly approved their request, which was just what the junior ministers had expected to happen."[16]

Thus, the king's two archrivals were erased from the political arena. This cleared the way for his next move, the importation of the *dharma*.[17] He recruited a sympathetic attendant to travel to India in search of a Buddhist master. No mere scholar would do; the most lauded pundit imaginable was required for the king's court. The best candidate was identified as Santaraksita, Head Abbot of the University of Nalanda.[18] Santaraksita accepted the position and traveled north to Tibet. Once safely ensconced within the royal household, Shantarakshita organized a curriculum of intense study in which he instructed "the basic Buddhist philosophy and ethics to a small group assembled by the king."[19]

The Bonpo ruling class watched in dismay while, for four months, Santaraksita transmitted his teachings. Then, an unforeseen ally stepped forth to give voice to the Bonpos' silent outrage—an ally literally dropped from the sky: The gods unleashed a storm from hell.

Lhasa was particularly hard-hit. Lightning ripped into the temple of Marpori (site of the present-day Potala Palace), reducing it to rubble. Torrential downpours washed away the Phangtang Palace. Untold numbers of villages were subsumed by flashfloods. The greatest calamity, however, was that the country's annual harvest was destroyed.[20] Facing famine, the people sought out their shamans for an explanation and a means to propitiate their panic. Why were the sky gods so angry?

It was obvious. The gods were wreaking revenge on the king because he had imported the heretical teachings of Buddhism. In order to placate the demons' wrath, Trhisong Detsen must send Santaraksita and his entourage back to the sub-continent.

Given the ruined crops, Trhisong Detsen had little choice

Storm over Tibet.

but to back down for the time being. He agreed to deport the scholar and, for his part, Santaraksita saw the wisdom in the king's acquiescence. Santaraksita's life was now in danger—even with the king's patronage. He would leave immediately. But before departing, Santaraksita made a suggestion that would later change the entire course of Tibetan history: Santaraksita nominated a replacement during his absence: "There is a mantra adept called Padmasambhava who is, at present, the most powerful in the world. I will send him an invitation, and Your Majesty should do the same."[21]

It was a shrewd idea—in Hollywood terms, "a casting coup." From the Bonpo point of view, the savage spirits had to be subdued. Very well, why not produce a far greater magician than the Bonpos had yet witnessed, a man whose mystical talents were honed precisely for these kinds of demonic subjugations? Padmasambhava's reputation had already earned him a kind of cult status in Buddhist India—by many; he was called the "second Buddha." Given the

mystical tastes of the Tibetans, would they not also succumb to his charismatic tantric displays? Padmasambhava embodied "the ideal apostle of Buddhism among an extremely primitive and violent people as the Tibetans then still were. More than a master of spirituality and asceticism, he was a mind-boggling miracle-worker with a clever knack for slaking the thirst for prodigies, miraculous cures, shamanic oracles, and impressive prophecies so prevalent"[22] in that era.

And it should be remembered that empirical science played no role in eighth century Asia. Manifestations of magic neither contradicted nor conflicted man's experience of the "real" world. People simply lived in an atmosphere of the marvelous. If someone was said to have super-human origins, no one jumped through hoops in order to accept it as fact. It is with this in mind that Padmasambhava's life will be related, since so much of what was written about the historical figure was folded into devotional testimonies of his otherworldly status.

PADMASAMBHAVA TAKES ON THE BONPOS

In Sanskrit, Padmasambhava means "lotus-born," a Buddhist idea charged with significance. The lotus symbolizes absolute purity—a flower conceived in sludge yet managing to emerge untainted by its murky origins. Buddha adopted the lotus as a metaphor for a kind of Immaculate Conception: The practitioner of Buddhism begins his metaphysical journey swamped by worldly suffering, but if motivation is correct and skillful means are perfected, he or she will journey upward and eventually reach the open sky of enlightenment.

Padmasambhava self-arose at the age of eight, on top of a magnificent lotus, in the middle of a lake, in full view of his earthly father, the King of Uddiyana.[23]

Was he, as Santaraksita suggested, the "second Buddha"? Certainly, like the Buddha, Padmasambhava was a prince who forsook family and throne in favor of an ascetic's existence. He wandered through India meeting with, and garnering all the teachings of, the greatest teachers of his age. Along the way, his prodigious acts of magic captured the devotion and the imagination of many followers.

The most popular image of him is not of a humble ascetic but rather of a mighty lord ensconced upon a magnificent lotus

Padmasambhava, lotus-born.

throne emerging from a lake. He is draped in the five color silks of a prince. He is adorned in jewels and, in the crook of his left arm rests a *khatvanga*, a flaming trident representing his tantric powers. A closer look reveals that two human heads and a skull are impaled on the khatvanga. Unlike images of the Buddha, whose eyes are slightly downcast in deep meditation, Padmasambhava's eyes look directly into the viewer's eyes. Clearly, this is a personage who demands respect. He could be unimaginably compassionate but he could, in a split second, also transform into a wrathful manifestation should the need arise.

One story relates that, when extremists challenged his teachings, he defeated them in debate and, when they subsequently cursed him, he "brought down a mighty thunderbolt which . . . set fire to their city."[24]

Another story tells of a Turkish king who invaded the Buddhist world by boat—a huge armada of 500 ships. Padmasambhava "raised his index finger in a menacing gesture and the five hundred vessels sank in the water."[25] His purpose in life was to benefit sentient beings and nothing would stand in his way to achieve that goal.

Upon receiving Santaraksita's (and King Trhisong Detsen's) invitation, he traveled across the Himalaya, subjugating all the Tibetan Bonpo deities along the way. He melted snow-massed mountains, he caused alpine lakes to boil, he pierced demons' eyes, he flew into the sky and created avalanches, he arrested the wind and created heat spells that transformed the Tibetan earth into molten iron. One by one, Padmasambhava fought, tamed, and ultimately transformed the Bonpo retinue of deities into a pantheon of Buddhist "protector gods," thereby creating the unique flavor of what was to become the Tibetan Buddhist register of deities.

right: A wrathful form of Padmasambhava.

ཧཱུྃ། ན་མོ་གུ་རུ་བྷྱཿ བདག་ལ་ཡཤེས་པ་ཞེས་པ་རྣམས་བཞུགས། སོགས་བཤད་པ་རྣམས་བཤད་དོ།

The monarch receives a teaching in humility: King Trhisong Detsen's first encounter with Padmasambhava.

PADMASAMBHAVA MEETS KING TRHISONG DETSEN

PADMASAMBHAVA MET THE KING some forty miles southeast of Lhasa, not far from the Brahmaputra River.[26] In the "tamarisk forest of Trakmar,"[27] a dozen kilometers west of present-day Samye, the 20-year-old king got his first taste of the great Indian's super-human powers. The year was 762 A.D.

The king was accustomed to being accorded the honor of prostration when someone encountered his presence. Padmasambhava saw no need for such submissive behavior. "I am a yogin who has reached attainment and, since I am invited to be the king's master, he will pay homage to me!"[28] The king had no such intention and a standoff ensued. Padmasambhava

listed his various accomplishments and concluded by saying, "Your lungs are inflated with your great dominion. I will not prostrate to the king of Tibet, but I pay homage to the clothing you wear." He then raised one hand from which a fiery ray of light exploded, scorching the young king's gown. King Trhisong Detsen fell to the ground in newfound respect.[29]

Padmasambhava was then escorted to the king's palace where he was feted and officially beseeched to consecrate the foundation ground of Samye. Padmasambhava consented to the plan but cautioned that there still remained recalcitrant local deities who had not been subdued. He climbed the nearby mountain of Hepori and proceeded to wage a supernatural war on the native gods. Casting a spell in a bowl of onyx, he thereby subjugated the haughty spirits, binding them by oath to protect—from here on out—the Buddhist religion. "In a glorious voice he ordered them to sublimate their pride, and, by performing a dance of indestructible reality in the sky, he blessed the site."[30]

In the meantime, Santaraksita had returned from India and joined King Trhisong Detsen and Padmasambhava at the site of the future Samye. (If the Bonpo ministers voiced any concerns, it was not recorded.) Santaraksita was named head abbot of Samye. In accordance with the abbot's orders, "the foundations were laid following the model of Odantapuri,"[31] a once-famous (no longer extant) monastery in Indian Bihar. The full name given to Samye was *Migyur lhungi dubpai Tsukla-khang,* meaning "the Temple of Unchanging Spontaneous Presence" or "Glorious and Spontaneous Fulfillment of Boundless Aspiration"—a mouthful in any language. In Padmasambhava's book, *Legend of the Great Stupa,* his pet diminutive for Samye is "The Inconceivable." And inconceivable it was. The chronicles include a series of miraculous events that occurred during the building of Samye, and its ambitious blueprint would prove to be unlike any Tibetan monastery to follow—a suitable pedigree for an abstract that was based on nothing less than the universal mandala.

Padmasambhava flies above
the valley to create Samye's
boundaries while the king
watches below.

THE SIGNIFICANCE OF MANDALAS
IN THE CONSTRUCTION OF SAMYE

Put in its simplest terms, a mandala is a diagram or pictorial representation of a three-dimensional universe used as an aid for Buddhist meditators. In its most common form it is symmetrical, concentrated about a center, divided into four quadrants of equal size with four corresponding "entrances." The central structure is then encircled by concentric walls.[32]

As a visual aid, it works as a kind of metaphysical blueprint to the innermost recesses of the human psyche. During meditation, every detail of the mandala should be kept in the practitioner's mind in a state of "radiant presence. . . .

Each mandala is meant to be set up and flowed through, stage by stage, around its layout, beginning with its eastern or southern quadrant and ending at the center."[33]

Depending on an individual's needs, these spiritual maps serve to explore a person's predispositions as well as the *abandonment of self,* a fundamental Buddhist ideal: The concept of "I" can only lead to jealousy, ignorance, and anger—aggregates that, in turn, result in an endless series of reincarnations into the world of human suffering.

The variety of mandalas and the Buddhist teachings based on them are innumerable. For the purposes of discussing

In a cave on Chimphu Mountain, Padmasambhava instructs the king on the inner meaning of mandalas.

Samye and its architectural layout, it will suffice to concentrate on the mandala of Mount Meru, the primordial home of the Tibetan gods.

Mount Meru is visualized as a heavenly palace "with a central room, courtyards, galleries, and walls with gates open to the four directions."[34] But this celestial mansion, with its divine residents, is also placed in context with its attending universe. Beginning from the outside of the mandala, suspended in space are the seven Joyless Realms of Great Wailing, Great Darkness, Fire, Smoke, Swamp, Sand, Water and Thorns; rising out of this is the Realm of Desire (the human realm); above this towers the Realm of Form (residence of the gods); surmounting it all is the Formless Realm. Geometrical shapes represent the continents that wash around the universal ocean while the sun and moon flank the earthly domain. The entire cosmos is girthed by seven mountain chains appearing as a single wall.[35]

The architects Padmasambhava and Santaraksita wanted Samye to be more than just Tibet's first monastery. Using the Mount Meru mandala as a template, Samye would be designed as a cosmic mandala—"the comprehensive expression of the architecture of enlightenment."[36]

Because of the metaphysical nature of the compound, many rites had to be performed to consecrate the ground. In an elaborate ceremony, Padmasambhava "made the magic-circle of Dorje Phurba with coloured stone-dust"[37] and conjured up the five Dhyani Buddhas. Then the Guru created several incarnations of himself, some of whom entered the Mandala, while some flew up into the sky."[38] The shadows cast from above created the outline of Samye, which the king and Santaraksita, valley-bound, marked out with tape.

Padmasambhava remained in meditation. Humans began the foundation while supernatural powers "rolled down rocks from the mountain side into the valley. What the gods and demons built during the night exceeded what the humans built during the day."[39]

There remained the problem of wood, a large quantity of which would be necessary to build the structures. "The country to the south of Samye was then, it is said, inhabited by the savage 'kLa-klo' tribes, which the Tibetans . . . termed nagas [serpent deities]."[40] Padmasambhava, it seems, had failed to bind these spirits by oath and so, through the powers created by a seven-day meditation, subdued, then extracted the nagas' promise to—from here on out—do everything they could to assist in the construction of Samye.

The mandala of Mt. Meru rising above the cosmos.

Padmasambhava consecrating the ground of Samye with his purba.

King Trhisong Detsen and Shantarakshita overseeing the floor plan of Samye.

Deities assist in the construction of Samye.

Padmasambhava subdues the naga spirits.

Partially finished Samye: Outlying buildings represent aspects of the cosmos.

A naga solved the wood problem. "A naga, having transformed himself into a white man on a white horse, came into the presence of the king and said, 'O king! How much wood do you need for building Samye? As I will supply you with all you want.'"[41] The nagas also produce vast amounts of gold to be used for ornamentation and sculptures.

The construction of Samye got underway without further obstacles. Its construction "progressed like a child growing to manhood."[42] Mount Meru began to take shape in the Tibetan valley.

"Just as the palace of the gods crowns Mount Meru, so the great Central Temple with three stories roofed in the three distinct styles of India, China and Tibet formed the centre of [Samye]."[43] Radiating away from the central axis, attendant structures began to take shape: There were "four major and eight minor temples symbolizing the continents, and two additional temples representing the sun and the moon."[44] Four mammoth *stupas*[45] arose and strategically punctuated the mandala: A white stupa in the southeast, a red stupa in the southwest, a black stupa in the northwest, and a blue stupa in the northeast.[46] The complex was finally enclosed "by a lofty circular wall about a mile and a half in circumference, with gates facing the cardinal points."[47] Around the entire length of this wall, crowning the ledge, over 1,000 three-feet-high stupas were placed.

In the meantime, the most arrogant of all the Tibetan spirits had not, as yet, been brought into the Buddhist fold. His name was Pehar Gyalpo, chief of the Five Ferocious Kings, and Padmasambhava concentrated all of his considerable powers in subduing this god. His efforts proved successful and he transformed Pehar into the "head of the entire hierarchy of protective spirits."[48] Later, a special temple was built in Samye to honor Pehar and his retinue of *dharmapalas*, protector deities. As an added precaution, Padmasambhava placed sacred vessels within various chapels through which Pehar could be "contacted" should the need arise.[49]

Celebration of the completion of Samye. The outlying wall is to be visualized as circular.

MANDALA OF BEAUTY ACTIVATED
INTO A COMPLEX OF INDUSTRY

Whether the construction took five years or, as some would have it, 12 years, the consecration of the compound was a dazzling celebration. According to Padmasambhava, "the gods came in the revelation of their wisdom, suffusing lights blazed, cymbals sounded spontaneously . . . while the gods rained down flowers and the Serpents presented offerings of jewels. . . . All-healing nectar fell from the sky three times, to bring virtue and happiness to the Land of Tibet."[50]

"The completion of Samye inspired the king with great confidence that Tibet could indeed become a Buddhist land, despite the initial difficulties he had faced."[51] He erected a pillar to the left of the main entrance of the *utse* (central temple) and had it inscribed with a declaration that Buddhism was the official religion of Tibet.

However, all was still not as harmonious as the king supposed. Dissatisfaction within the aristocracy, who refused to sever the ties with the ancient Bonpo rites, became vociferous and had to be addressed. Padmasambhava observed, "In their jealousy, the ministers of Tibet had been thwarting our efforts to fulfill the king's wishes."[52] He and Santaraksita conferred and considered returning to their own country.[53]

Upon hearing this, King Trhisong Detsen begged them

King Trhisong Detsen's pillar.

to reconsider and stepped up his efforts to neutralize aristocratic resistance. He opened up the royal coffers to bring in additional help. Twelve novices from Kashmir and seven young native Tibetans were selected to become the first monks.[54] Santaraksita ordained them in an elaborate ceremony. Then the king "selected 108 young Tibetans to study Sanskrit and train as translators in India. Among them was Vairotsana, who visited many lands and brought important lineages to Tibet."[55] Translators were invited from China as well. None, however, were as prodigious as the famous Pandita Vimalamitra, brought from India at Padmasambhava's request.

The effect of this influx of scholars was astounding. Suddenly, Tibet went from being an intellectual wasteland to *the* most important academic hub in Asia: "Samye became the center of a systematic translation effort unparalleled in history."[56]

Even for a non-believer, it must have been an amazing sight to wander through Samye's highly populated, multilingual complex. Walkways radiated and intersected one another connecting temples to libraries to translations schools to meditation halls—everywhere the assiduous hubbub of learning and scholastic enterprise vied for one's attention and praise.

Monastic discipline was taught in one building, Chinese masters conducted philosophical exercises in another; grammars and dictionaries were being written and printed in

Vairotsana.

Vimalamitra.

Jampa Ling, site of the "Great Debate."

Inside the Samye compound facing north: to the left is the "Blue" stupa; the central building is Pehar Ling, chapel of the dharmapalas and Samye's original treasury.

Padmasambhava meditating in Chimphu cave.

Padmasambhava with his 25 disciples in a Chimphu cave.

yet other locales while the treasury was safeguarded in the fearful chapel of Pehar: Within its dark confines, wrathful dharmapala statues, the boom of low-voiced drums and sonorous chanting could be heard 24 hours a day.

What chance did the Bonpo malcontents have to voice objections—given the pervasive, almost delirious timbre of Buddhist activity now firmly established at Samye? By rural Tibetan standards, Samye was a major metropolis. And there was no turning back the king, particularly since his far-flung armies were providing Tibet with unprecedented wealth and political stability. The Chinese Emperor, Hehu Ki Wang, for example, was terrified of Trhisong Detsen and was obliged to pay him an annual tribute of 50,000 rolls of silk. The king secured military alliances all over the map. In the distant east, he had formed a treaty with the King of Siam while, to the far west, his allied forces reached as far as the Oxus River.[57] Everything he touched, it seemed, turned to gold. And his broad-minded handling of the Bonpo situation was hard to deny: It was true that he had limited "certain activities of Bon teachers and even banished some of them. But he was very careful to protect valuable Bon teachings, preserving them as treasures."[58] Bonpo detractors fell silent under the sway of the King's enthusiasm, his even-handed mandates, and the sheer physical preponderance of Samye itself.

Nor did Trhisong Detsen make the mistake of resting on his laurels. Lest anyone suppose that the creation of Samye satisfied the king's enthusiasm for Buddhism, he ordered the construction of additional meditation centers throughout central Tibet. He literally took his new religion "on the road": He mounted his steed, sought out local chiefs and discussed the *Dharma* with them, patiently explaining the basic outline of Buddhist beliefs and the reasons why such a system was advantageous to the Tibetan people.[59]

Eventually, the maturation of Padmasambhava's disciples and the continuing expertise of Head Abbot Santaraksita allowed Padmasambhava to spend less time at Samye and more time on the 17,500 ft. peak of Chimphu, five hours away to the northeast. The upper contours were riddled with caves that offered the perfect sanctuary for isolated meditation, as well as breathtaking views of the Brahmaputra River five thousand feet below. The length of his stay there is a matter of debate, but it would appear that, in the years that ensued, when the King or Padmasambhava's disciples took instruction from the great mystic, it was in the warrens of Chimphu.

At some point during this lengthy retreat, tragedy struck the royal household. King Trhisong Detsen's daughter, Pemasel, fell ill and died. According to Padmasambhava's account, the king and his three sons "came to me at Chimphu with the three-day-old corpse . . . and begged me for the

Sangye Yeshi, disciple of Padmassambhava.

Namkhai Nyingpo, disciple of Padmassambhava.

initiation"[60] for resurrection. He gave the bereaved a full explanation of the *Epitome of the Ocean of Dharma* and other secret instructions, after which Trhisong Detsen's daughter miraculously came back to life.

The mountain became a magnet for disciples of Padmasambhava—a kind of companion *mandala* to Samye below—and its steep topographical contours were likened to the petals of an unfolding lotus made evident to all practitioners whose skills were adequately advanced. Padmasambhava's "mature disciples were initiated into the all-embracing *Mandala of the Unity of the Mind*"[61] and other esoteric teachings. It was on Chimphu that they achieved enlightenment and "freed themselves from the karmic cycle of rebirth."[62] Each disciple revealed, and became famous for, a different sign of achievement. Sangye Yeshe, for instance, could shatter rocks with his *phurba* (a ritualistic dagger); Gyalwa Chokyang could transform his body into a raging fire; Kharchen Tsogyal could bring forth water of eternal life from rocks; and Namkhai Nyingpo could ride on the sun's rays.[63]

As the centuries passed, Chimphu would become a preeminent retreat center for mendicant monks and nuns and, for the laic Buddhist, as important a destination for sacred pilgrimage as Samye itself. The stupa of the great Nyingma master Longchenpa still stands on Chimphu—the site of Longchenpa's enlightenment. And a small monastery has been built around and over a cave that Padmasambhava considered one of the five places of realization."[64]

Central temple of Samye.

THE GREAT DEBATE

BEFORE HE DIED, Santaraksita predicted that eventually there would come a conflict between the two schools of Buddhism then spreading in Tibet. One was the teaching that enlightenment was an instantaneous realization that could be attained only through complete mental and physical inactivity; this system was being spread by the Chinese monks. The other, which Santaraksita had introduced, maintained that enlightenment was the result of a slow, gradual process, requiring study, analysis, and good deeds. Santaraksita instructed that when the time came, his disciple, Kamalasila, should be invited from India to defend the Indian system of Buddhism.

"The king . . . called for the debate, and it was held at Samye over a two-year period (792–94). Hoshang, a Chinese monk, defended the 'instantaneous system' and Kamalasila, the 'slow system.' At the end of the debate, Kamalasila was declared the winner, and the king issued a proclamation establishing the new religion as the orthodox faith for Tibet. The document was written in gold letters on blue paper and was kept in the court records."[65]

The significance of the victory of the Indian system over the Chinese system can hardly be overestimated. Given the political events of the time, this furthered Tibet's position that it was, in no way, reliant on Chinese influence. In the event, a great celebration was held at Samye and the king himself is said to have sung the following lyrics:

With great toil have I gathered this treasure
And I am happy to spend without measure
In spreading the faith of the Buddha,
Gleaned from the land of India.
This temple, not built by human hand,
Has grown by itself from our sacred land.[66]

THE PASSING OF THREE FOUNDERS

B<small>Y THE TIME</small> S<small>ANTARAKSITA PASSED AWAY</small>, the monastic system at Samye was firmly established but Padmasambhava stayed on. He prophesized to the king that, in the future, Buddhism would be persecuted from many quarters. "Intending that the teaching of the secret mantra should not vanish, nor the genuine blessing be weakened or adulterated by sophistry, and that disciples should gradually appear, he concealed countless treasures"[67] called "terma," which would be revealed to the proper disciples sometime in the future.

But for the time being, Tibet was at the zenith of its powers. King Trhisong Detsen's ability to assemble the best around him, his ineluctable vitality, and his dauntless optimism—all continued to serve the Tibetan people well until his death at the age of 69. An inscription on a stele near Chongyas gives testimony to his greatness:

> King Trhisong Detsen . . . You have carried out everything that your father and grandfather desired for the peace and welfare of our country and the improvement of our places of worship . . . The extent of your magnificent Empire has brought greatness to Tibet. We are a happy people, peacefully practicing our

heart. Not only are you generous and kind to your human subjects, but to all living creatures as well.[68]

How long Padmasambhava remained at Samye and Chimphu after the king's death is debatable, though it is certain that he remained for some time as advisor for the king's son, heir to the throne. It is most likely that he remained in Tibet "for an additional five years and six months."[69]

"When master Padmasambhava was about to leave . . . the king, ministers and subjects of Tibet begged him to stay on. But he declined. To each of them he gave detailed instructions, and precepts concerning loving kindness. Then, riding on a lion, or on an excellent horse, he set out from the summit"[70] and flew to the "glorious Copper-coloured Mountain . . . and there he resides, ruling in his eight emanations over eight ogre islands, reaching the eight transmitted precepts concerning the eight means for attainment and other doctrines. . . . He continues to dwell, even now, as the regent of the spontaneous presence of the final path; and so will he remain, without moving, until the dissolution of the universe."[71]

Padmasambhava departs.

Samye today, as seen from Mount Hepori.   51

PART II

APPROACHING THE MANDALA

Willows on the northwestern shore of the Tsangpo (Brahmaputra) River.

WHO'S VISITING WHOM?

ANY WESTERNER who has found himself investigating a place on foot, only to discover that he has stumbled onto something *more*—an inkling, a brief vision perhaps, a intuition that the chambers of a lock have silently retreated because the proper key has been inserted—that person has a notion of what a pilgrimage in the Tibetan context means. The sensation is one of having rubbed shoulders—however briefly—with the hidden soul of a place. It is an intensely personal moment, palpable but probably impossible to share with others. You are safe in its environs. You feel unblocked. You are uncharacteristically still. Then, like a Tibetan pilgrimage, the exploration becomes interactive: Once you have achieved the precise coordinates, the place transforms into a map of your own position within yourself. In other words, the place places *you*.

Lest the reader get the impression that a pilgrimage is heavy-going somber stuff, it should be noted that Tibetans are nothing if not fun-loving people. A pilgrimage implies a big adventure. It may take months to trek to a sacred location. No matter how arduous, a pilgrimage *is* a vacation, a big dose of tourism, a departure from a Tibetan's normal life, and a great opportunity to observe other regions and the people who inhabit them—there will be many amusing stories to relate once the pilgrim returns home.

But the underlying goal is not obscured.

Tibetans are spiritually ambitious Buddhists.

Pilgrimages are a means of accumulating spiritual merit—this Tibetans take seriously because, always, the reward is enlightenment. A pilgrimage is a "returning to the center, a way of realizing the central meaning of the Buddha's life and teachings."[72]

If you ask Tibetans what pilgrimages they hope to make, Samye is likely to be listed for a variety of reasons. Samye was where Buddhism took root in Tibet. It is the site of the first monastery. All of the early translations of Sanskrit texts were written within its circular wall. Nearly all of the great masters spent time there. Many are said to have achieved enlightenment at Samye.

And there is also this: When a person dies and enters into the *bardo*,[73] his or her first transmigratory stop will be Samye. Pilgrims come to Samye to offer clippings of their hair so that lamas may conduct rites to help ensure that their bardo will not be delusional. Visiting Samye is one way of getting a diplomatic passport to the next life.

✵   ✵   ✵

These days, if you are coming from Lhasa, you can take a bus that will drop you off at the Samye ferry in a matter of hours. At this juncture, the Tsangpo River, which will be the next leg of the journey, is a magnificent tranquil expanse—shallow and glistening—nearly a half-mile's distance from the ferry landing to the far shore. One has the impression one is looking at a lake rather than a river. Its silent current heads eastward, always following the northern wall of the Himalaya. Eventually, it will escape into Assam and spill down into the alluvial plains of northern India.[74]

While waiting for the boat to return from the northern shore, pilgrims park their belongings away from the mud embankment; squat in groups; snack on dried yak cheese, yak-jerky, and wash it down with cups of salty yak-butter tea. Local dogs keep watch at a respectful distance: There might be an aberrant crumb left here or there, but whatever abundance pilgrims have, it is saved for the keepers of the mandala, the Samye monks, and nuns.

The ferry, a rude flat-bottom contraption, returns to the Lhasa side.

Thirty or so pilgrims scramble aboard. Rough-hewn planks serve as seats for people and bundles alike. The Tibetans, normally a loquacious lot, become hushed. Perhaps they are reminded that they are now guests in the famous

Yarlung valley, residence of the ancient kings (including Trhisong Detsen, the monarch who established Samye). Perhaps they focus on a beacon that can just be made out—a saffron-colored flickering: Though the main temple of Samye is still obscured from this distance, the sunbeams darting off the gilded roof give away its remote location.

It is an hour's journey, and everyone settles into the pattern of the gentle rocking of the boat. The helmsman negotiates lengthy shoals that striate the shallows. Old women bring out their *malas*[75] and incant prayers to the sky vault. Calloused hands dangle over the side and figure eight through the ruffled surface. Stalwart mountain men toss barley over their shoulders, one grain at a time, while muttering ancient mantras their fathers taught them as children.

The northern landing comes into view while the mountains behind it, rising 18,000 feet, begin to take on a more impressive stature. A boy on the bank moves crabwise, back and forth, trying to second-guess where the boatman will throw him the rope.

Once disembarked, the pilgrims climb into the rear of an open truck that softly maneuvers the sandy nine-kilometer track weaving and undulating toward the temple complex tucked well into the valley and away from the river. The truck passes Zurkardo, the boulder-choked precipice where five white *stupas*[76]

punctuate the skyline. This is the spot where King Trhisong Detsen first met Padmasambhava and where his robe was singed by the guru's magical display of fire. Pilgrims nudge one other. Cupped hands are held against foreheads in attitudes of devotion.

The valley nestles at 12,500 feet above sea level. Something strange is noticed: Snow-supplied rivulets trickle down into the basin and create a sub aqueous lushness that does not quite fit in with the hostile topography. Willows, barely fields, and verdant pastures are growing here. A vagrant pony peeks around an ancient tree bole. Invisible birds trill within a dappled glade. A yak briefly looks up before returning to its languid foraging, the bell around its neck tossing out one desultory ting. Gnarled pear and peach orchards also punctuate the drive. All of this casually dispersed fertility, at this altitude, begins to feel otherworldly: an oasis nestled within a lunar landscape. And the closer one gets to the Samye complex, the more surreal the sensations. Everything about the place suggests a geomantic power spot. One begins to understand that Samye was not just randomly selected to embrace the first Buddhist monastery in Tibet.

The great circular wall, surmounted by 1008 stupas, comes into view. The truck veers to the left, following the wall's recumbent contours. Then the vehicle shifts into a lower gear, edges through the northern gate and bumps past various chapels, past the great blue stupa, and finally grinds to a halt in the central piazza spilling away from the main temple.

From this angle, the temple's complicated mass is almost too much for the eye to take in. There is a timeless majesty to its proportions. Its upper stories meet the sky in a variety of swoops and punctures. The green-tiled "guardhouses" along the rooftop suggest a golden fortress, as indeed it is. Not only is it a repository of priceless sacred objects, but it is a spiritual Fort Knox as well. Ancient teachings and mythic holy men evolved within its secret corridors, fostering a system that has remained constant for 1,200 years.[77]

The pilgrims do not seem to take much notice. They unceremoniously drop from the truck, heft their bundles over their shoulders, and scatter into twos and threes—an outspread of bifurcated devotion—not toward the main temple but away from it. Perhaps they wish to save the best for last.

Many of them head back to the eastern main gate of the great circular wall. In a clockwise direction, following the inner curve of the enclosure, the devotees make a circuit of the complex—at least once, but just as likely, many times. Along the way, they approach freestanding walls in which long rows of prayer wheels protrude from stone niches. Each prayer wheel contains thousands of mantras. If activated by spinning, the prayers will fly out into the universe for the benefit of all sentient beings. A happy clacking ensues as the pilgrims set the brass cylinders in motion. (Not all of the wheels are well oiled; some require considerable effort to launch. The Tibetans, never ones to shrink from physical exertion, put their shoulders to the task with a delightful lack of solemnity.)

Orbits within orbits.

This rotational process—the circumambulations, the spinning—is called *chora*[78]—a walking rite that symbolically "turns the wheels of Buddha's teachings." This is one practice that all Tibetans can do on their own regardless of their religious education (or lack thereof), and they do so with great relish. Chora has a kind of giddy, dizzying logic of its own. If done for an extended period of time, the effect is trance-like and exhilarating at the same time.

The chora takes the pilgrims past many chapels. In the miniature quadrangles of these piles, tin cans of geraniums, mallows, roses, marigolds, and dahlias abound—vibrant and clashing hues that echo the travelers' party colored clothes. Some of the structures—particularly the ones built during Pad-masambhava's time—demand a closer investigation. Yak butter candles will be lit and offerings made at the altars of *Tsangmang Ling* (once the monastery's printing press), *Arya-palo Ling* (Samye's first building), *Dragyur Gyagar Ling* (the original translation school), *Jampa Ling* (site of the Great Debate), and *Pehar Ling* (the chapel of wrathful protector deities), among others.

Ling means "island"—a metaphor crucial to the mindset of Tibetan practitioners. Humans are born again and again in the Sea of Samsara (world of suffering) until they reach enlightenment. By making chora around these "islands," the practitioner is paying heed to his own oceanic misery, which is (he must remind himself) no different from the suffering of all sentient beings. In other words, lings act as advisors, prompting the correct path for Buddhists to take, thus helping them to break their endless cycle of reincarnations.

Likewise, the four great stupas of different colors—white, red, black and blue—preside over this circumambulation and take on a life of their own. Just below their golden spires, the all-seeing eyes that are carved in bas-relief stare down at the pilgrims. The eyes *follow* the pilgrims as if to encourage them to look within themselves for the proper motivation.

✳   ✳   ✳

Only after the pilgrim has paid homage to these outer buildings is the mendicant prepared to return to the central courtyard and enter the *Utse*, the main temple.

To the left of the Utse entrance stands a pillar with an inscription written by King Trhisong Detsen proclaiming that with the completion of this temple, Buddhism has become the official religion of Tibet. The stele reminds one of how important—from an historical viewpoint—this structure truly is. The unique architecture of the Utse, a combination of Tibetan, Indian, and Chinese edificial elements, pays tribute to the confluence of far-flung ideas—a philosophical symphony that somehow managed to funnel its way into this valley, creating an entirely new identity for Tibet. Looking up at the seductive interplay of golden roofs, one is struck by a sense of reduction: Self-importance simply dissolves.

The pilgrim prostrates three times, then disappears into the vast darkness of the ground floor chapel. This is the vortex of the Samye mandala, the "hub of the world, around which the universe unrolls and revolves."[79]

The nave is cavernous and cold. Here and there, a shaft of light angles down from the high rare windows. Butter lamps blaze in tight clusters on the main altar, behind which the central gold Buddha towers: incrusted with turquoise and coral and supreme in his equanimity. *Thankghas*[80] framed in silk brocade depend from unseen rafters. Steel blue smoke—juniper incense—intermittently catches the light as it curls upward. Basso profundos in the maroon robes of monks chant among the shadows. In a different corner, keeping a separate beat is the legato boom of an elevated drum.

Rows of deities look down upon the pilgrims as if to acknowledge that, yes, the answers reside within these walls and that there are many more unseen deities who are waiting to help practitioners along their way. "Go ahead," they seem to encourage, "investigate this ascending labyrinth." Take this absurdly steep stairwell. Look into that doorway. *Everything within the mandala is here to help you*. From the ground floor, "the way leads up to finer, subtler spheres of the uppermost storey. It is like a journey along the spiritual path, a climbing from the world of space and time to the timeless omnipresence of cosmical consciousness."[81]

❋   ❋   ❋

For many Tibetans, the surrounding environs of Samye are just as important as the monastery itself.

Chimphu Mountain, in particular, is a must for most pilgrims. This is where Padmasambhava spent much of his time during the construction of Samye. Lengthy stints in claustrophobic caves provided the perfect settings for his detached meditative practices—a system that is still emulated among the hermits who inhabit the Chimphu warrens. Monks and nuns alike live in these cells—many for three years or more—retreating from the outside world in order to meditate without distraction.

These anchorites' unfettered existence is made possible by the generosity of pilgrims. What meager food, clothing, and other necessities they receive come from the visitants who scale the mountain with precious provisions strapped to their backs. Like spinning the prayer wheels— *I spin you, you propel prayers in moral support of me*—feeding the cave dwellers is a common sense trade-off: *You, in your cold cavern, meditate on behalf of all sentient beings—I, a sentient being, will help you survive so that you can continue to help me and my kind.*

From Samye, Chimphu is a half-day trek. It begins through flat, sandy tracts with sparse vegetation. An occasional lizard may dart into view but, otherwise, the terrain seems hostile to fauna. After a few hours, one heads north between the extended arms of two mountains. The fold leading upward to the crest of a mountain, surprisingly green from this perspective, is Chimphu.

The climb is gradual at first. Ice cold brooks encased in velveteen collars of grass must be waded or jumped over. Moist ditches and spongy turf provide the perfect environment for thirsty butterflies and Tiffany-colored dragonflies. Orange-red ladybugs pepper the dwarf encampments of buttercups, nettles, and brambles. Magpies and thrushes flit here and there as if to show one the way.

As the ascent steepens, new flora clusters around the ever-deepening path. Fragrant barriers of juniper embellish surrounding embankments. The sandy floor gives way to gravelly dirt and tufts of barberry. The Tibetans sun seems to intensify as the trail reaches upward. After a thousand foot climb, the path widens, then levels into a modest promontory. The pilgrim reaches a human enclave.

It is a hermitage for nuns. The first ropes of prayer flags, of which one will see thousands more higher up, are draped in lazy swags between squat stone buildings. To the right is the main chapel around which nuns in maroon robes and shaved heads make chora while whirling handheld prayer wheels. It is a good place to drop one's pack and look back to where one started off. The mighty Tsangpo River already seems quite far below in the hazy distance.

Bass horns suddenly blare from inside the nunnery, intentionally clashing with one another. Harmony is not the goal of these unwieldy, ten-foot instruments. They are attention-getters utilized to punctuate the oral readings of scripture. The pilgrims take off their shoes, step over the stone threshold, prostrate three times, then work their way around the seated rows of women—mostly young—who sing in unison with the "leader" of the texts. A nun or two may smile in one's direction, but they remain undistracted from the task at hand. After leaving a small container of yak butter at the base of the altar (this donation will be used by the nuns to fuel the butter lamps), the pilgrim returns outside and continues the ascent.

From this point on, the pitch of the trail becomes more vertical. Thorny bunches of wild white roses, six feet high, close in around the switchbacks, each turn holding its own surprises. A yellow tattered curtain of arnica is in bloom. A massive bolder blocks the way with multicolored mantras inscribed across its surface. A Tibetan family unfurls a string of prayer flags that they have brought all the way from home and which they will now stretch above the pathway. Thrushes chatter in the undergrowth. Edelweiss begins to show up here and there, as do diminutive fir trees. A covey of snow pheasants scrape at a dirt patch, then scurry into a briar tunnel disguised by wild rhubarb. And all the while, the air grows thinner.

Eight hundred feet above the nunnery, another upland plateau is achieved. This open grassy table marks the beginning of the Chimphu caves. The first cave encountered, and one of the most famous, is Padmasambhava's "Vajrakilaya" cave. It sits, hump-like, at the very edge of a precipice. Prayer flags droop over the top like bird plumage. A manmade entrance has been devised. There is even a window behind which the ancient caretaker monk reads his sacred texts. A crude rock altar indicates where the Great Master conducted his tantric meditations. The pilgrim is welcome to practice here.

The plateau is narrow. The mountain becomes almost vertical from here up. The trail splits into numerous smaller paths, each leading to a group of lesser caves now inhabited by anchorites. Pilgrims leave humble offerings at the entrances of these caves, often without the dwellers aware of the visitation. Thank yous are not necessary up here. The act itself is the reward. This is and always has been a mountain of miracles. Giddiness comes into play. By now, the rarified air can induce an almost hallucinogenic quality to the trek. One is not certain if one's shortness of breath is due to elevation or to the ever-increasing proximity of the gods.

At 16,000 feet, one reaches a ledge on which a monastery has been constructed around the most famous of Padmasambhava's caves. Inside sits an elaborate altar. An old, goitered nun presides over the inner sanctum, making sure the votives always remain burning. This is where Padmasambhava brought King Trhisong Detsen's daughter, Pemasel, back to life. She died at the age of eight and the distraught king brought her body up to Chimphu. "Padmasambhava wrote the syllable NR (source of human existence) on Pemasel's breast in vermilion . . . and caught hold of her consciousness with the sharp hook of his contemplation. When she could again open her eyes and speak," he gave her empowerments that would continue on into many rebirths.[82]

The pilgrim goes back outside. The view from here is surely one of the most spectacular on earth. The terrain is as wild as the wind that swooshes up from the valley in great unexpected gusts. Overhead, countless prayer flags whip and snap like the wings of the cranes famous for migrating over the Himalaya. Higher still, high above the altitudinous monastery, cloud formations—pilgrims of an adamantine sky—scud by in accelerated fashion only to disappear over the crest of the peak. White stupas can be seen along the uppermost ridge. This is where wild dogs and vultures await the next sky burial.[83] The trekker will make *that* pilgrimage at a later date.

For now, there is only a sense of floating. Perched on this ledge—for all the world like a hawk surveying his kingdom—the traveler feels a profound satisfaction in being here.

> With my own two feet, I earned this view.
> But who's viewing whom?

Like all holy spots, Chimphu is redolent with unseen spirits who observe the observer. And all around this mountain slope are sacred places where the great masters came and achieved enlightenment. Tibetans are brought up on these Chimphu stories and know them by heart.

At the end of his life, for instance, Longchenpa came to Chimphu. He said, "I would rather die here than be born elsewhere. Here I will leave this worn-out, illusory body of mine."[84] And after he died, "there were limitless miracles, and the whole earth shook and resounded. His body was left undisturbed for twenty-five days, during which time the deities who rejoice in the teaching unfurled a canopy of rainbow light, and caused a shower of flowers to fall."[85]

Jigme Lingpa also achieved enlightenment on Chimphu; likewise for Karmapa III, and many others. Yeshe Tsogyal, Sakya Jungne, Nyang Ral Nyima Ozer, Sangye Lingpa, Pema Lingpa, Thangtong Gyalpo performed miracles here—the list goes on and on.[85] No pilgrimage in Tibet can boast a better "Who's Who" of famous yogis and yoginis.

There is no place for name-dropping or snobbism or reflected glory in Buddhism, of course, but it is difficult not to feel a little intoxicated by the ghost-like proximity of enlightened lamas who once practiced here.

Elongated shadows begin to redefine the jaw-dropping panorama. The late afternoon sun fall reminds the pilgrim that there is still a long trek back to Samye. Soon, it will be getting cold.

Why is it so difficult to leave?

Once attained, it is not easy to leave the home of the gods. There *is* something going on up here.

Reluctantly, the pilgrim heads back down the mountain. Perhaps a nugget of quartz, or a pheasant feather, or some other natural souvenir will be pocketed as a memento. Perhaps the memory alone will suffice.

Buddha said that everything is an illusion.

Perhaps the head abbot of Samye got it right when he told this author, "Once you've been here, you never really leave."

Rainbow over the southeastern shore
of the Tsangpo River.

Pilgrims pile in a truck that will take them to Samye.

A family from Lithang.

An astonishing lushness at 12,500 feet: pear orchards.

Grazing land abounds in this mountain oasis.

A monk shields himself from the fierce alpine sun.

The four Great Stupas of Samye come into view.

Young monks in a study group outside the main complex.

A young pilgrim sports distinctly non-Tibetan attire.

One of the many brooks that feed into the valley and contribute to its lushness.

The great circular wall with
its 1,008 stupas. The mountains
enveloping Samye rise to 18,000 feet.

Long rows of prayer wheels echo the outer perimeter of the Stupa Wall.

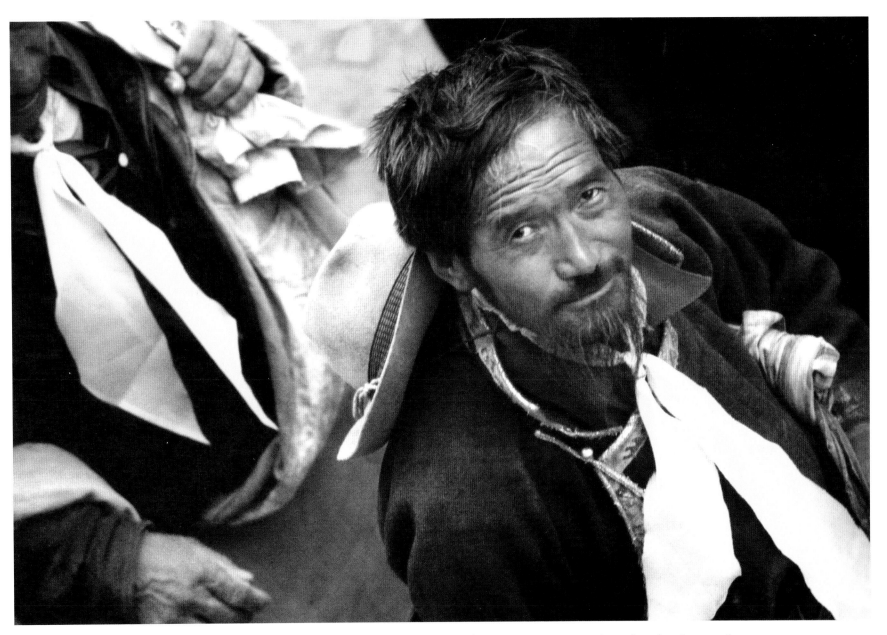

Pilgrims proudly wear the yellow khatags (ceremonial scarves) given to them by the Samye lamas.

The Moon Temple. Originally, its companion building, the Sun Temple, flanked the opposite side of the central Utse, thus creating the balanced iconography of the Mount Meru mandala. The Sun Temple was razed during the Cultural Revolution.

Jangchub Semkye Ling: one of four chapels representing the cardinal directions.
Semkye Ling is in the northern quadrant of the mandala.

The Great White Stupa.

Teenage pilgrim from Kham.

The Great Red Stupa.

Ten-gallon hats have been a fashion
staple for nearly a century.

The Great Black Stupa.

Pilgrim from Amdo.

Ceremonial stand on the northern side of the central piazza. High-ranking lamas are seated here during festivals and other important gatherings.

Utse with yak in foreground. Ponies and cattle also roam the Samye valley.

Aryapalo Ling, the chapel of the western direction and thought to be Samye's first building.

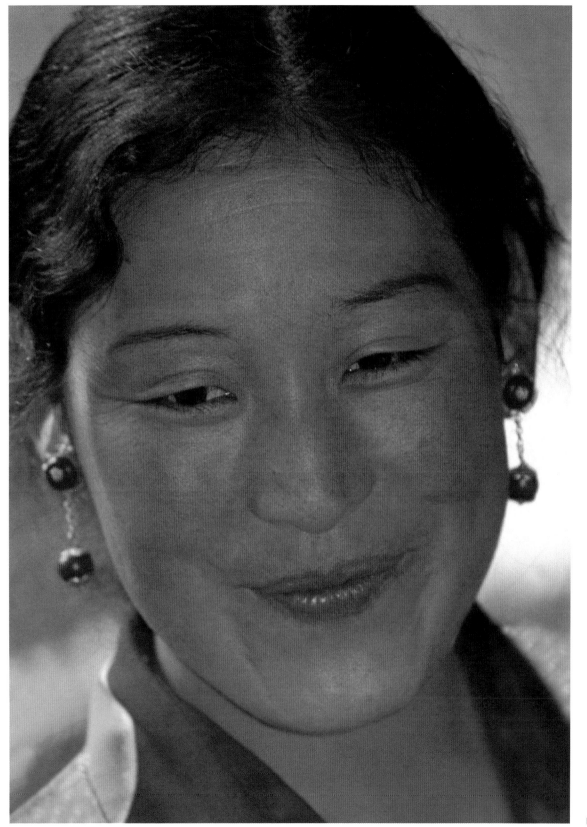

Pilgrim from Kongpo.

Monks don blue smocks when assigned custodian duties.

left: The U-shaped courtyard that surrounds the back of the Utse is lined with prayer wheels, thus offering pilgrims with yet another circuit for chora.

right: Main façade of the Utse. The haze is created by gargantuan incense pots stoked with smoldering juniper.

"Pilgrimage enacted with devotion turns the mind toward knowledge and parts the barriers erected by self-doubt and fear; admiration for those who showed the way to attainment awakens vision, generating love for all beings and an earnest wish to contribute to their happiness. Within this wider vision, pilgrimage takes on the quality of prayer; fusing a deep inner communion with the outer form of devotion, pilgrimage becomes a celebration of human potentiality, a way to participate in the . . . cosmic play of the fully awakened ones . . . the pilgrim experiences, however briefly, the thrust toward enlightenment that gives rise to an endless procession of Buddhas. With heart established in faith, the pilgrim returns from this journey to a world transformed into a stage for accomplishment."

TARTHANG TULKU

from *Holy Places of the Buddha*

PART III

ENTERING THE MANDALA

Entrances to the inner chambers of the mandala gain importance
by the elaborately designed doors. No two doors are the same.

Statues in the main altar room are both peaceful and wrathful.
This protector god has been honored with stacks of
silk-wrapped sadhanas (sacred texts).

The cavernous proportions of the main
altar room dwarf rows of benches,
where monks come to practice.

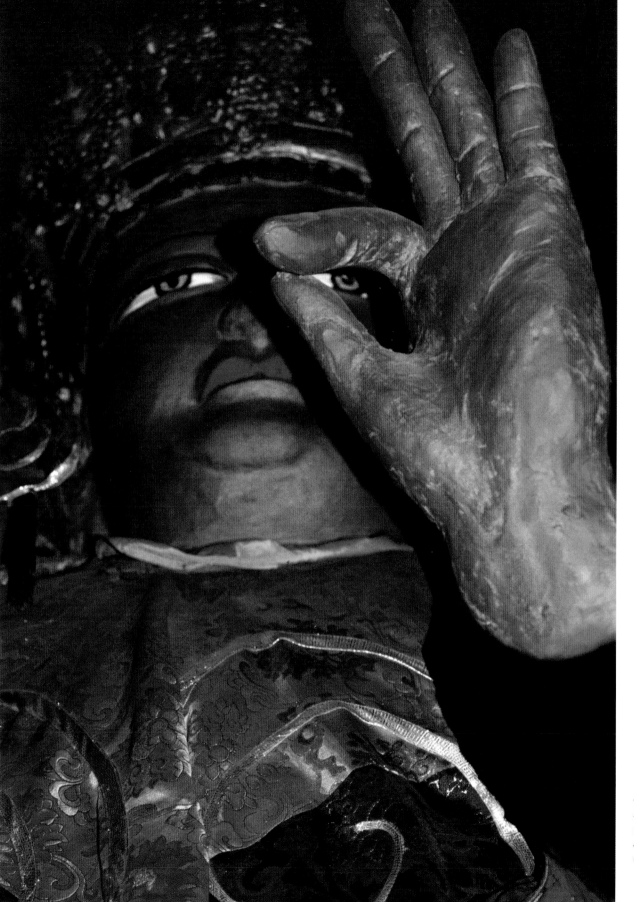

Twelve bodhisattvas statues lead to the main altar. A bodhisattva is one who attains enlightenment on behalf of all sentient beings rather than just oneself.

Shakyamuni Buddha, the historical Buddha, commands
the central position behind the main altar.

Huge yak butter lamps with multiple wicks illuminate the darkness.

Statue of Padmasambhava.

Vivid appliqué of "wish-fulfilling jewels" hangs between pillars.

Row of bodhisattvas.

Background paintings often echo the statues placed before them.

A monk stands beneath a 14-foot three-dimensional mandala.

Golden Heruka, protector god.

Entrance to Pehar Ling, a chapel of wrathful deities. The impermanence
of life and the transitory bardo of death are meditated on within these walls.

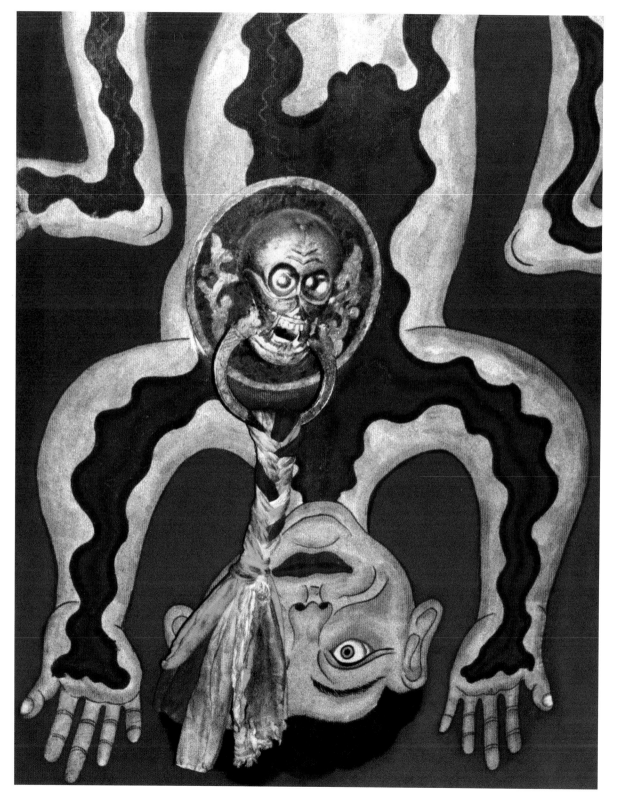

A flayed human decorates a door at Pehar Ling.

Monks light votives in front of a semi-wrathful emanation of Padmasambhava.

Beams entwined with "nagas," serpent spirits, that watch over a corridor in Pehar Ling.

119

Garishly-colored "tormas," butter sculptures, are created
for special practices—in this case, for wrathful deities.

121

Dorje Drollo.

Red "wrathful" door detail in Pehar Ling.

The impermanence of man worked into architectural elements.

Khampa pilgrim.

A seldom-seen gallery off the main temple houses some of the most splendid murals found in Samye. The entire history of Tibetan Buddhism is painted on its two floors.

Padmasambhava peeks behind a woodpile.

Anchorites in snowbound caves.

The history of the building of the Potala,
home of the successive Dalai Lamas.

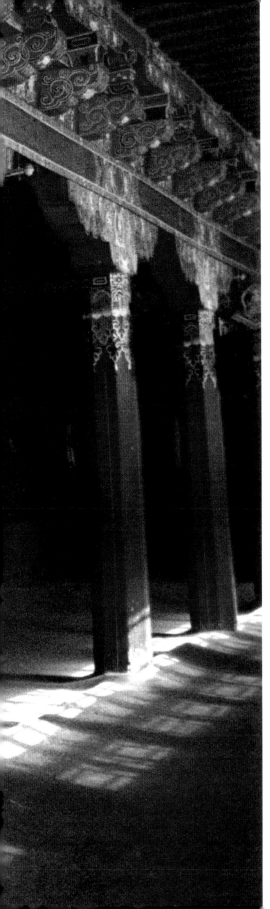

Second floor entrance in the Utse.

An opening in the second floor labyrinth.

A monk with incense performs a rite in a second floor chapel.

Few windows provide illumination in the dark complex.

Third floor gallery.

The galleries that wrap around the entire third floor are lined with famous personages, saints, and deities connected with the history of Tibetan Buddhism.

Ceiling mandala.

Nanam Yeshe.

Samantrabhadra with his consort.

Mandarava, Padmasambhava's Nepalese consort.

Yeshe Tsogyal, Padmasambhava's Tibetan consort.

Sogpo Lhapal.

Dorje Drollo.

Hayagriva.

Kalachakra with consort.

Khorlo Dompa.

Vajradhara with consort.

Peaceful emanation of Padmasambhava.

Southern view of surrounding mountains. In the left foreground can be seen
the lower rise of Hepori, where Padmasambhava subdued the local deities.

A brief stairway leads to a secret chapel dedicated to Amitabha, the primordial Buddha. This is the only site in Samye that the photographer was not allowed to shoot.

Off limits to pilgrims: the golden roof of Samye.

The Great Red Stupa as seen from the roof.

156   Sky guardian: the Tibetan version of a gargoyle.

One of four rooftop
"guardhouses."   157

First snow (shot in early September) salts the northern peaks.

A "certo," a rooftop ornamentation, proclaims the victory of Buddha's teachings.

The head abbot of Samye.

Padmasambhava's instructions to the Buddhist clergy:

"Monks of future generations who journey on the path of liberation, be free from selfish, temporal aims and embark on the path of emancipation. Leave your parents, family, and friends and be free from attachment. Shave your heads, don the robes of the Dharma and attain excellence. Serve your preceptors, teachers, and elder monks. Wash and sweep your dwelling place nicely. Set out the offering in a beautiful way . . .

"Pious women who become nuns, cut your attachment to men and observe the precepts with purity. Engage in teaching and study and gather as much virtue as you can. Recite prayers and be energetic in circumambulation and prostration. Keep the rules of the precepts free from deceit and hypocrisy.

"Male and female monastics of Tibet, when you become an object of other people's respect . . . do not engage in acts of self-aggrandizement. Do not brag about your Dharma practice. Do not pretend greatness, booming like an empty drum . . . since the main point is to cherish everyone with compassion."

PART IV

WITHIN THE MONKHOOD

Each year, a new "leader" is selected among the monks
and lamas to supervise group chantings. Here, the
newly-chosen is ceremoniously "enthroned."

In the Samye treasury, there are priceless relics dating back to the era of Padmasambhava: Santarakshita's skull, a turquoise statue of Buddha Shakyamuni, the personal seal of King Pehar and Vimalamitra's walking stick, among others. Here, the head abbot has ordered the lamas to bring out the great seal of Padmasambhava. Using hand-ground vermilion ink, the monks are making an imprint on a silk scarf to be given to a highly honored visitor.

Monk holding tray of three
tormas (butter sculptures).

Debate College with
Utse in background.   183

Westerners wandering into a debate college for the first time might very well think they had stumbled into a martial arts school. Young men who have been paired off seem demonstrably in conflict with one another. One takes a passive seated position, while the other paces in front of him, making accusations. The aggressor enunciates every word, his manner belligerent. His index finger jabs at the air, then comes dangerously close to the other monk's face. He storms away and then, just as dramatically, pivots around, lurching toward his opponent for all the world as if to strike him soundly across the face.

The accused seems remarkably unimpressed by all the histrionics. If given the chance, he will insert a remark that infuriates the other monk all the more. At some point, he will have had enough, raises his hand in disgust and waves off the aggressor's argument.

Each afternoon at 4 P.M., the monks gather at the debate college to enact this conflict. Their debate lama will have supplied them with a new philosophical topic in which they are to explore the pros and cons. After 30 minutes, the opponents trade places, the "accused" becoming the angrily dancing aggressor.

Of all the subjects in a monk's education, debating is surely one of the most popular. Not only does it give the students an opportunity to put their knowledge on display, but it also gives vent to these young men's physicality. The improvisational aspect of the practice gathers audiences—debate in the Tibetan world is synonymous with entertainment. When dignitaries visit the monastery, it is not unusual to stage a debate—the best of the school's orators showcased. Witticisms abound. The laughter from the audience illustrates one of Tibetan Buddhism's primary tenets—that practice should always be a "joyful" effort.

191

"Having laid the foundation for Samye, I have thus fulfilled the aspiration of the Tibetan king. I will now remain in meditation for three months and three days at the upper retreat of Chimphu."

PADMASAMBHAVA

Thus, many disciples, including King Trhisong Detsen and Yeshe Tsogyal, sought out Padmasambhava among the mountain caves of Chimphu. It was here, 5,000 feet above the Tsangpo River, where their understanding of the Buddhist texts matured and their practice bloomed into enlightenment.

PART V

ABOVE THE MANDALA

Setting off for the ascent. The contents of the bundles on the pilgrims' backs—tea, barley meal, and yak butter—will be distributed as offerings to the cave-dwelling monks and nuns above.

Three pilgrims from the Kongpo region preparing to scale the holy mountain.

Old nun spinning her prayer wheel. She is the caretaker of a cave
said to have been the retreat of Yeshe Tsogyal, consort and biographer
of Padmasambhava. Yeshe Tsogyel is one of the preeminent figures
in the Tibetan canon of enlightened beings.

Pilgrim from the Chamdo region.

Many of Padmasambhava's teachings to his disciples were conducted in Chimphu caves.

Hung by pilgrims, this canopy of prayer flags
serves as a sun shield for a young anchorite.

Half way up, the mountain levels off at the site of one of the most famous caves, Padmasambhava's "Vajrakilaya" retreat. A virtual beehive of adjacent dens house long-term retreatants—monks and nuns alike.

Devotion is anything but moribund.

Blue gentian and other rare flora flourish in the higher regions of Chimphu.

Padmasambhava's "Vajrakilaya" cave.

Levitation is one form of "mundane" magic said to be perfected through advanced meditative practices—mundane because, according to Buddha, anyone can learn such feats: Real enlightenment is evinced by displays of profound compassion.

above: Three stupas signifying the path that leads up to the saddleback of Chimphu where sky burials are performed.

right: Padmasambhava often counseled King Trhisong Detsen in the warrens of Chimphu.

Farther up the mountain is the small monastery built around yet another cave used by Padmasambhava. Miraculous events occurred here, including the resurrection of King Trhisong Detsen's eight-year-old daughter.

Steep ascent to the monastery. The pilgrim has now reached an elevation of 16,000 feet.

Padmasambhava with three disciples.

The nunnery on the mountainside is the home of 80 practicioners.

Longchenpa's stupa: where the great adept achieved enlightenment.

above: A pilgrim from Derge enjoys the view.

right: Bhutanese artists have been commissioned to create several sculptures
for the Chimphu monastery. Here, a clay Buddha dries in the sun.

The caretaker nun of Padmasambhava's shrine.

The view from Chimphu at 16,000 feet.

PART VI

PRECARIOUS PRESERVATION

THAT SAMYE STILL EXISTS is something of a miracle. Several major fires from earlier centuries altered the face of the original Samye complex, and the mere withstanding of 1,200 years of harsh Tibetan weather has also taken its toll.

Far more devastating was Mao Tse-tung's "Cultural Revolution." Of the 6,000 monasteries that flourished in Tibet, prior to the Chinese Communist invasion in 1950, a mere dozen remained more or less intact by 1970. Samye fell under the latter category.

The Red Army pulled down Samye's magnificent golden roof and shipped the precious metal back to mainland China.

The monks were expelled, imprisoned, or murdered. Some of Samye's temples—including the Utse—were turned into barns. To this day, many enclosures in Samye exhibit a "high-water mark"—a rubbing away of priceless frescos where yaks and other livestock brushed against the walls of their confines. The statues that were not destroyed on the spot were trucked out, only to reappear as art for sale on the Hong Kong black market.

The paintings were particularly hard hit. Many murals were systematically desecrated. When painting deities and other sacred personages, the final element a Tibetan artist includes is the eyes. This is a very important moment, usually accompanied by the prayers of a lama—in this way, the image is now "activated" and suitable for worship. The Red Army, well aware of this practice, simply gouged out the deities' eyes as a time-saving device.

But the most devastating loss—at least from a Buddhist standpoint—was the irreplaceable loss of ancient religious texts—many of which dated back to more than a millennium and were the only known copies. Usually, on-site bonfires took care of the despised libraries, although forcing monks and nuns to use the texts as toilet paper was not an uncommon form of Chinese entertainment.

Barbaric vandalism is no longer sanctioned by the communist party. By the 1980s, a certain amount of "contained" reconstruction was allowed to take place. In many cases, seed money for monastic projects was even provided for by Beijing. This is not to suggest that the communists had or have any interest in returning Buddhism to its former glory. Buddhism is still the "enemy of the people." The change in policy occurred because the Chinese government came to understand the economic and propagandistic value in tourism. Tibetan monasteries are now promoted as showcases for the communist regime's newfound "respect" for the culture of an indigenous people. It is the Disneyland approach.

At the time of this writing, Samye has not yet reached the sad state of affairs of Lhasa, where Chinese vendors now sell Coca-Cola on top of the Jokhang Cathedral, the holiest building in Tibet. Samye is still primarily visited by Tibetans. But things are rapidly changing. A bridge over the Tsangpo River is near completion, thus clearing the way for effortless day trips from the capital so that westerns, in large groups, can spill out of tour buses, take the prerequisite snapshots, and get back to their Lhasa hotel in time for cocktails. What effect this will have on Tibetan pilgrims can only be imagined.

Samye's plight is the same as all Tibetans' plight: finding a way to preserve an ancient culture without igniting the ire of the Chinese.

Before the Chinese invasion, there were thousands of monks and nuns living in Samye. The government now allows only 180 monks to live at the monastery and 80 nuns to live in the hermitage on Chimphu.

Locals have surreptitiously filled in the gouged eyes of deities with flour paste in an effort to prevent further deterioration of the paintings—but the monks do not dare re-paint the eyes in fear of raising the Communists' wrath.

King Trhisong Detsen's palace, filled with amazing murals and architectural details, has been "appropriated" by the Chinese. Some of the chambers have been turned into granaries. Other rooms have become storehouses for scrap metal. Elegantly executed Buddhas now stare down at fuliginous tractor parts and rotten tires where altars used to glimmer.

Cadres stationed in a building, once a chapel, across the courtyard from the Utse spend most of their time watching Chinese TV. When they do venture out among the Tibetans, it is usually manifested by a kind of desultory parade to the local shops. However, their uniforms still serve as a reminder that at any given moment, the central government could close down Samye without further notice.

Perhaps most telling of all is what the Communists have done to the great circular wall of Samye: In Chinese characters spray-painted across its exterior, they have saluted themselves for "liberating the oppressed people of Tibet." Seldom, if ever, has graffiti been more tragically eloquent.

Ironically, in the eighth century, Padmasambhava predicted this dark future. He foretold that it would occur "when the iron bird flies."

There is no doubt that dreadful times will come.
Tibet will be split and its districts divided.
Even Samye will be destroyed.
The age of weaponry will advance.
Tantric yogis will die at the knife blade.
And soldiers will be guarding the outer doors.

It is unimaginable that Tibetans will enjoy any real independence in the near future. Only when that day arrives will there be a secure future for Samye monastery.

One of the ineluctable tenets of Buddhism is that everything changes, that nothing is permanent.

May change come soon to the Land of the Snow Lions.

A Tibetan toddler dressed in a
Chinese vest. The subtle shifts in
Tibetan culture are everywhere.

Vandalized
"palace" painting.

Vandalized "Yellow Hat" painting.

The king's palace is now used as a granary.

King Trhisong Detsen's palace
in its new incarnation as a
Chinese appropriated junkyard.

The "rubbed-away" evidence from livestock that was housed within the walls of the king's palace.

Interior of Jampa Ling after it was turned into a stable during the cultural revolution.

Communist propaganda spray-painted across the Great Stupa Wall.

PART I

1. Maraini, Fosco. *Secret Tibet*, The Harvill Press, London, 1998. Maraini also argues that since the Bonpos' conception of the universe is a dualistic struggle between good and evil, Bon's origins are "definitely derived from Iranian and Manichaean sources."

2. *Ancient Tibet*, Dharma Publishing, California, 1986.

3. Ibid.

4. Some historians record his reign as occurring during the fifth century A.D., but it seems more probable that he was born circa 173 A.D.

5. Dudjom Rinpoche. *The Nyingma School of Tibetan Buddhism: Its Fundamentals and History*, Wisdom Publications, Massachusetts, 2002.

6. Tsepon W. D. Shakabpa. *Tibet: A Political History*, Potala Publications, New York, 1984.

7. Dudjom Rinpoche. *The Nyingma School of Tibetan Buddhism: Its Fundamentals and History*, Wisdom Publications, Massachusetts, 2002.

8. Maraini, Fosco. *Secret Tibet*, The Harvill Press, London, 1998.

9. Ibid.

10. Elchert, Carole. *White Lotus: An Introduction to Tibetan Culture*, Snow Lion Publications, New York, 1990.

11. Tsepon W. D. Shakabpa. *Tibet: A Political History*, Potala

Publications, New York, 1984.

12 Maraini, Fosco. *Secret Tibet*, The Harvill Press, London, 1998.

13 *Ancient Tibet*, Dharma Publishing, California, 1986.

14 Ibid.

15 Tsepon W. D. Shakabpa. *Tibet: A Political History*, Potala Publications, New York, 1984.

16 Ibid.

17 The teachings of Buddha.

18 Later destroyed by the Muslim invasion. It was located in present-day Bihar, India.

19 *Ancient Tibet*, Dharma Publishing, California, 1986.

20 Dudjom Rinpoche. *The Nyingma School of Tibetan Buddhism: Its Fundamentals and History*, Wisdom Publications, Massachusetts, 2002.

21 Ibid.

22 Maraini, Fosco. *Secret Tibet*, The Harvill Press, London, 1998.

23 Located in or near the Swat Valley, present-day Pakistan.

24 Dudjom Rinpoche. *The Nyingma School of Tibetan Buddhism: Its Fundamentals and History*, Wisdom Publications, Massachusetts, 2002.

25 Ibid.

26 *Tsangpo* in Tibetan.

27 Dudjom Rinpoche. *The Nyingma School of Tibetan Buddhism: Its Fundamentals and History*, Wisdom Publications, Massachusetts, 2002.

28 Yeshe Tsogyal. *The Lotus-Born*. Yeshe Tsogyal was Padmasambhava's Chinese consort. She became an adept herself, reaching the highest levels of enlightenment and became Tibet's first woman teacher as well as Padmasambhava's biographer.

29 Ibid.

30 Dudjom Rinpoche. *The Nyingma School of Tibetan Buddhism: Its Fundamentals and History*, Wisdom Publications, Massachusetts, 2002.

31 Ibid.

32 Brauen, Martin. *The Mandala, Sacred Circle in Tibetan Buddhism*, Serindia Publications, London, 1997.

33 Rawson, Philip. *Sacred Tibet*, Thames and Hudson, London, 1991.

34 Tarthang Tulku. *Art of Enlightenment, A Perspective on the Sacred Art of Tibet*, Dharma Publishing, California, 1987.

35 Brauen, Martin. *The Mandala, Sacred Circle in Tibetan Buddhism*, Serindia Publications, London, 1997.

36 Cook, Elizabeth (editor). *Crystal Mirror Series Vol. 12, The Stupa: Sacred Symbol of Enlightenment*, Dharma Publishing, California, 1997.

37 Waddell, L. Austine. *Tibetan Buddhism with its Mystic Cults, Symbolism and Mythology, and its Relation to Indian Buddhism*, Dover Publications, New York, 1972.

38 Ibid.

39 Yeshe Tsogyal. *The Lotus-Born: The Life Story of*

Padmasambhava, Shambhala Publications, Massachusetts, 1993.

40 Waddell, L. Austine. *Tibetan Buddhism with its Mystic Cults, Symbolism and Mythology, and its Relation to Indian Buddhism*, Dover Publications, New York, 1972.

41 Ibid.

42 Guru Padmasambhava. *The Legend of the Great Stupa*, Dharma Publishing, California, 1973.

43 Ibid.

44 *Ancient Tibet*, Dharma Publishing, California, 1986.

45 *Stupa:* "chorten" in Tibetan. Stupas are an important staple of Tibetan architecture. Originally, they were probably constructed in imitation of Buddha's dome-shaped tomb in Kushinagar, India. They evolved into reliquaries for the remains of saints, Buddhist scripture, and other holy artifacts. On the most esoteric level, stupas are viewed as three-dimensional diagrams of the universe and therefore qualify as mandalas.

46 Blue and green are somewhat interchangeable in the Tibetan artist's palette. Thus, Samye's "blue stupa" is often as not rendered a dark teal.

47 Waddell, L. Austine. *Tibetan Buddhism with its Mystic Cults, Symbolism and Mythology, and its Relation to Indian Buddhism*, Dover Publications, New York, 1972.

48 Avedon, John F. *In Exile from the Land of Snows*, Alfred A. Knopf Publications, New York, 1986.

49 Ibid.

50 Guru Padmasambhava. *The Legend of the Great Stupa*, Dharma Publishing, California, 1973.

51 *Ancient Tibet*, Dharma Publishing, California, 1986.

52 Guru Padmasambhava. *The Legend of the Great Stupa*, Dharma Publishing, California, 1973.

53 Ibid.

54 *Ancient Tibet*, Dharma Publishing, California, 1986.

55 Cook, Elizabeth (editor). *Crystal Mirror Series Vol. 12, The Stupa: Sacred Symbol of Enlightenment*, Dharma Publishing, California, 1997.

56 Ibid. "Through the close collaboration of panditas and Tibetan lotsabas, the entire Vinaya was translated within a single generation, together with nearly 750 Sutras, Dharanis, and sastras, including all the major Prajna-paramita Sutras and the extensive Ratnakuta and Avatamsaka Sutras."

57 Tsepon W. D. Shakabpa. Tibet: A Political History, Potala Publications, New York, 1984.

58 *Ancient Tibet*, Dharma Publishing, California, 1986.

59 Ibid.

60 Guru Padmasambhava. *The Legend of the Great Stupa*, Dharma Publishing, California, 1973.

61 Ibid.

62 Ibid.

63 Ibid.

64 Cook, Elizabeth (editor). *Crystal Mirror Series Vol. 12, The Stupa: Sacred Symbol of Enlightenment*, Dharma Publishing, California, 1997.

65 Tsepon W. D. Shakabpa. *Tibet: A Political History*, Potala Publications, New York, 1984.

66 Ibid.

67 Dudjom Rinpoche. *The Nyingma School of Tibetan Buddhism: Its Fundamentals and History*, Wisdom Publications, Massachusetts, 2002.

68 Tsepon W. D. Shakabpa. *Tibet: A Political History*, Potala Publications, New York, 1984.

69 Dudjom Rinpoche. *The Nyingma School of Tibetan Buddhism: Its Fundamentals and History*, Wisdom Publications, Massachusetts, 2002.

70 Ibid.

71 Ibid.

PART II

72 Tarthang Tulku. *Crystal Mirror Series Vol. 9: Holy Places of the Buddha*, Dharma Publishing, California, 1994.

73 Literally, "interval" or "space." The intermediate state between death and the next rebirth. During this interval, souls have many opportunities to make right and wrong decisions, which will affect the quality of their next incarnations.

74 In India, the Tsangpo is called the "Brahmaputra"; literally, "Brahma's son."

75 Rosary beads.

76 Stupas are domed monuments, usually holding sacred relics of an accomplished yogi. The shape embodies an elaborate symbolism. On one level, stupas are part of a world mandala—a three dimensional diagram of the Buddhist universe. On another level, they are mandalas unto themselves representing, among other things, the body, speech, and mind of the historical Buddha.

77 *"The Temple which is an Unchangeable Mass"* is Samye's full name, a moniker that Padmasambhava simplified by nicknaming it *"The Inconceivable."*

78 Literally, "circle" in Tibetan.

79 Tucci, Guiseppe. *To Lhasa and Beyond: Diary of the Expedition to Tibet in the Year 1948*, Snow Lion Publications, New York, 1987.

80 Scroll paintings.

81 Tucci, Guiseppe. *To Lhasa and Beyond: Diary of the Expedition to Tibet in the Year 1948*, Snow Lion Publications, New York, 1987.

82 Dudjom Rinpoche. *The Nyingma School of Tibetan Buddhism: Its Fundamentals and History*, Wisdom Publications, Massachusetts, 2002.

[83] Tibetans never bury their dead. The common way of disposing of corpses is startlingly unsentimental. The body is taken to a charnel ground where it is hacked to pieces and thrown to carrion eaters.

[84] Dudjom Rinpoche. *The Nyingma School of Tibetan Buddhism: Its Fundamentals and History*, Wisdom Publications, Massachusetts, 2002.

[85] Ibid.

[86] Ibid.

Beer, Robert. *The Encyclopedia of Tibetan Symbols and Motifs*. Berkeley: Shambhala, 1999.

Bell, Charles. *Tibet Past and Present*. Delhi: Motilal Banarsidass, 1992.

Changchub, Gyalwa and Namkhai Nyingpo. *Lady of the Lotus-Born*. Boston: Shambhala, 1999.

Cook, Elizabeth. *Holy Places of the Buddha*, edited by Tarthang Tulku. Berkeley: Dharma, 1994.

Getty, Alice. *The Gods of Northern Buddhism*. New York: Dover, 1988.

Jackson, David Paul. *A History of Tibetan Painting*. Vienna: Verlag der M-Vsterreichishe Academie der Wissenschaften, 1996.

Jigmei, Ngapo Ngawang, et. al. *Tibet*. New York: McGraw-Hill, 1981.

Kvaerne, Per. *The Bon Religion of Tibet*. Boston: Shambhala, 1995.

Lizhong, Liu. *Buddhist Art of the Tibetan Plateau*, edited and translated by Ralph Kiggell. San Francisco: China Books, 1988.

Olschak, Blanche Christine and Geshe Thupten Wangyal. *Mystic Art of Ancient Tibet*. Boston: Shambhala, 1987.

Perkins, Jane. *Tibet in Exile*. San Francisco: Chronicle Books, 1991.

Rawson, Philip. *The Art of Tantra*. London: Thames and Hudson, 1978.

Sinha, Nirmal C. *Tales the Thankas Tell*. Gangtok: Sikkim Research Institute of Tibetology, 1989.

Waddell, L. Austine. *Lhasa and its Mysteries*. New York: Dover, 1988.

Willis, Michael. *Tibet: Life, Myth, and Art*. New York: Stewart, Tabori and Chang, 1999.

Yeshi, Pedron, ed. *Cho-Yang* Vol. 7. Dharamsala: Norbulingka Institute, 1996.

Mikel Dunham spent his childhood on a Black Angus cattle ranch in the foothills of the Ozark Mountains. After college, he lived several years in New York City as a gold trader in the Lebanese bank empire run by Edmond Safra. He spent the next few years in Paris, Munich, and one year on the island of Crete.

After returning to America, he married and moved to Connecticut where he and his wife, Margaret, had two sons.

Mr. Dunham's writing career was preceded by his success as an artist. Represented by the Alexander F. Milliken Gallery in Soho in the 1980s and early 1990s, his box-assemblages and three-dimensional photographic collages were widely exhibited, including one-man shows in Europe, New York, and other major cities in the U.S.

In 1989, Mr. Dunham made the first of many treks in the Himalaya. This was a turning point in his career. After returning to New York, he took refuge with Tibetan lamas and became the last student of the late thankgha master, Pema Wangyal of Dolpo, spending years learning how to paint in the Tibetan manner with mineral pigments and 22 carat gold. This led to his commission to paint the murals for a newly constructed Tibetan temple in Sarnath, India—one of the eight major pilgrimage sites for Buddhists.

The Dalai Lama subsequently consecrated the temple in a 1997 ceremony. Mr. Dunham's next major project was for a Tibetan temple being erected in upstate New York where he served as artistic director for the massive murals commissioned therein.

During the 1980s and 1990s, Mr. Dunham also managed to write the Rhea Buerklin Series of murder mysteries published by St. Martin's Press.

In 2000, Dunham was sent to Tibet by the Vajrakilaya Foundation to photograph Samye, Tibet's first monastery. The foundation's main concern was to record on camera every mural that still remained intact, fully understanding the fragility and uncertainty of Samye's future, given the Communist Chinese regime. Dunham was given full access to Samye's secrets and treasures, many of which had never before been photographed. The spirit of the place so captivated Dunham that he made a second trip, concentrating on Samye's environs and the Tibetan pilgrims whom he met along the way. Jodere Group's *Samye: A Pilgrimage to the Birthplace of Tibetan Buddhism* is the product of those two trips.

Mr. Dunham is currently finishing a book titled *Buddha's Warriors: The True Story of Khampa Resistance, and the Fall of Tibet*—a history based on interviews with resistance fighters which, for the last seven years, he has conducted in various Central Asian refugee camps. Putnam Penguin will release the book in 2004.

Mr. Dunham currently resides in Santa Monica, California, with his wife of 25 years, Margaret.

S A M Y E
NEEDS YOUR SUPPORT

THE WILLIAM HINMAN FOUNDATION is an organization with a program, FRIENDS OF SAMYE, that has been specifically designed to support the 1,200-year-old monastery. By becoming a member of FRIENDS OF SAMYE, your charitable contributions will be used exclusively to help preserve and enrich this very important monument, the birthplace of Tibetan Buddhism.

If you would like to know more about FRIENDS OF SAMYE and the William Hinman Foundation, you may visit their website at *http://williamhinmanfoundation.com* or email them at *friendsofsamye@williamhinmanfoundation.com*.

We hope this Jodere Group book has benefited you in your quest for personal, intellectual, and spiritual growth.

Jodere Group is passionate about bringing new and exciting books, such as *Samye,* to readers worldwide. Our company was created as a unique publishing and multimedia avenue for individuals whose mission it is to impact the lives of others positively. We recognize the strength of an original thought, a kind word, and a selfless act—and the power of the individuals who possess them. We are committed to providing the support, passion, and creativity necessary for these individuals to achieve their goals and dreams.

Jodere Group is comprised of a dedicated and creative group of people who strive to provide the highest quality of books, audio programs, online services, and live events to people who pursue life-long learning. It is our personal and professional commitment to embrace our authors, speakers, and readers with helpfulness, respect, and enthusiasm.

For more information about our products, authors, or live events, please call (800) 569-1002 or visit us on the Web at www.jodere.com.